EDITOR:

OSPREY
MILITARY

MEN-AT-A   SERIES   275

THE TAIPING REBELLION 1851-66

Text by
IAN HEATH
Colour plates by
MICHAEL PERRY

First published in Great Britain in 1994 by
Osprey, an imprint of Reed Consumer Books Ltd,
Michelin House, 81 Fulham Road,
London SW3 6RB
and Auckland, Melbourne, Singapore and Toronto

ISBN 1 85532 346 X

Filmset in Great Britain by Keyspools Ltd
Printed through Bookbuilders Ltd, Hong Kong

Note on spelling
To avoid unnecessary confusion, I have opted to use the
same transliterations of Chinese words as were employed by 19th century authors. Readers will therefore
find Peking, not Beijing; Hung Hsiu-ch'uan, not Hong
Xiuquan; Kwangsi, not Guangxi; and so on.

Publisher's note
Readers may wish to study this title in conjunction with
the following Osprey publications:

MAA 95 *The Boxer Rebellion*

MAA 198 *The British Army on Campaign: 3
1856–1881*

MAA 224 *Queen Victoria's Enemies: 4 Asia*

Artist's note
Readers may care to note that the original paintings
from which the colour plates in this book were prepared are available for private sale. All reproduction
copyright whatsoever is retained by the publisher. All
enquiries should be addressed to:

Michael Perry
3 Quorn Close
Attenborough
Nottingham
NG9 6BU

The publishers regret that they can enter into no
correspondence upon this matter.

For a catalogue of all books published by Osprey Military
please write to:

The Marketing Manager,
Consumer Catalogue Department,
Osprey Publishing Ltd,
Michelin House, 81 Fulham Road,
London SW3 6RB

THE TAIPING REBELLION 1851–66

Taiping troops in action, from Augustus Lindley's Ti-Ping Tien Kwoh. Note the jingall crews at left.

The Taiping Rebellion was only the first, albeit the most dangerous, of a spate of insurrections against the ailing government of China in the mid 19th century. Between 1850 and 1877 the Moslems in the west and north-west of the country, the Triads and the aboriginal Miaou in the south, and the Nien and the Taipings in the east all took up arms against their Manchu overlords in a series of revolts that nearly brought the Ch'ing dynasty to an end. The catalyst for such widespread rebellion was China's humiliation by Britain in the Opium War of 1839–42, which had highlighted the impotence of her antiquated army. However, the inefficiency of the Ch'ing government had prepared the way, through a combination of overtaxation, corruption, official discrimination against minority groups and the administration's failure to match China's massive population explosion (from 125 million in 1736 to 432 million by 1852) with a proportionate increase in arable land.

The Taiping movement began as the *Pai Shang-ti Hui* (the Society of God-Worshippers), founded in Kwangsi province in 1846 by Hung Hsiu-ch'uan. A sickly individual of questionable sanity, Hung had become subject to visions which, having read a small amount of Christian literature, he chose to interpret as demonstrating that he was Jesus Christ's 'Divine Younger Brother', with God's mandate to govern China.

Hostilities between the God-Worshippers and local militia units broke out in October 1850, when the former took sides with the relatively newly-arrived Hakka people of Kwangtung and Kwangsi provinces (Hung was himself a Hakka) in a land-war with the Pen-ti population. Early successes in this local war, combined with an unsuccessful Imperialist attempt to destroy the God-Worshippers' camp at Chin-t'ien as a centre of local banditry, led to Hung's proclamation in January 1851 of his *T'ai-p'ing T'ien-Kuo* or Heavenly Kingdom of Great Peace, with himself as *T'ien Wang* (Heavenly King). His principal lieutenants were installed in December as the *Tung Wang* (Eastern King), *Si Wang* (Western King), *Pei Wang* (Northern King), *Nan Wang* (Southern King) and *I Wang* (Assistant King).

The ensuing civil war's first phase, lasting until March 1853, saw the Imperialist armies depending on the walls of their fortified cities for safety from theTaiping forces, who remained highly mobile and thereby retained the initiative. They advanced down the Hsiang valley, capturing city after city but always quickly abandoning their conquests and moving on. (No attempt was made to occupy captured territory permanently until much later.) Despite some setbacks – the *Nan Wang* and *Si Wang* were both killed during 1852 – the Taiping army had grown from some 10,000 to perhaps half a million by the time it arrived at Lake Tung-t'ing on the Yangtze. There the Taipings captured a massive Imperialist flotilla, and with this they were able to advance rapidly downriver, capturing Wuchang, Anking and other cities en route until on 20 March 1853 they took Nanking, the old capital of Ming China. Nanking became the capital of the nascent Taiping state.

The Taipings' seizure of Nanking may have been symbolic, but it seems almost certain that its strategic importance had also been recognised, since possession of Nanking and the debouchment of the Grand Canal into the Yangtze nearby effectively blockaded Peking by cutting it off from the fertile southern provinces which fed it. Nevertheless, establishing themselves here is generally regarded to have been a

strategic error. The consensus is that if the Taipings had marched against Peking at once, the Ch'ing dynasty would almost certainly have been overthrown. Instead, only a small contingent – perhaps 20,000 men – was sent on towards the capital in May. Even this succeeded in coming within three miles of Tientsin, before inadequate supply-lines, the severe cold of the northern winter and the want of cavalry (Taiping armies invariably consisting almost entirely of foot soldiers) obliged it to fall back, in February 1854.

The failure to send sufficient forces to the north resulted from the Taipings' need to defend their conquests, in particular their new capital. This was an onerous burden, which curtailed their earlier mobility. Thereafter their field armies had to be recalled to Nanking repeatedly to frustrate attempts at encirclement mounted from two Imperialist headquarters that had been established north and south of the Yangtze late in 1853, usually referred to as the Northern or Kiangpei, and Southern or Kiangnan Imperial Barracks. The Imperialist blockades were broken in 1856, 1858, 1859, and twice in 1860 (the Northern camp was overrun in September 1858, and the Southern in 1856 and again, decisively, in 1860). However, the Taipings' failure to break a renewed blockade in 1862 was to result in Nanking's eventual fall.

In the meantime the idealism and discipline of the Taiping movement's early days ended in internal strife. Recognised from the outset as military commander-in-chief, the *Tung Wang* or Eastern King, Yang Hsiu-ch'ing, steadily strengthened his position by claiming visions akin to those of Hung Hsiuch'uan. Eventually, in the summer of 1856, it became apparent that preparations for the transfer of power in the capital were afoot, but Yang's rival, the *Pei Wang* or Northern King, moved first, surprising and killing Yang and 20,000 of his supporters in a bloody two-week purge. Alarmed at this, Hung recalled his kinsman, the *I Wang* Shih Ta-k'ai, to the capital, but the *Pei Wang* attacked Shih's family, forcing him to flee for his life. It was not until November that Hung's own troops were able to regain control in the capital, defeating and killing the *Pei Wang* after two days of street-fighting. Shih Ta-k'ai subsequently

China in the mid-19th century

returned as head of government, but he was unable to get along with Hung and eventually struck out on his own into the Western provinces in 1857, taking as many as 50–70,000 Taiping soldiers with him. After campaigning with varying success in eight provinces, occasionally in alliance with regular Taiping Army units, he was eventually captured and executed by the Imperialists in 1863.

The purges of 1856 marked the beginning of the Taiping movement's decline, effectively eliminating its remaining capable leaders as well as a good part of its most experienced soldiery. Hung Hsiu-ch'uan henceforth trusted only members of his own family, and he installed them in most of the key governmental positions. At the same time, military operations assumed a mostly defensive character, after the relentless ebb and flow in the fortunes of both sides over the preceding years, when some cities had changed hands up to eight times. Taiping fortunes revived, however, with the promotion in 1857 of two talented military commanders – Li Hsiu-ch'eng, who in 1859 was made *Chung Wang* (Faithful or Loyal King), and Ch'en Yu-ch'eng, who became *Ying Wang* (Heroic King) – whom successive famines provided with a seemingly inexhaustible supply of soldiers. They operated virtually independently of the corrupt Celestial Court in Nanking, the *Chung Wang* fighting to the east of the capital and the *Ying Wang* to the west. It was by their efforts alone that the Imperialist blockade of Nanking was repeatedly broken in 1858–60. The 'Great Camp of Kiangnan' was finally destroyed in May 1860, and the besieging armies scattered.

The momentum was once again with the Taipings, and the *Chung Wang* set out on an Eastern expedition aimed not only at securing control of the Yangtze delta, but also at the capture of Chanchufu and Soochow on the Grand Canal and the seaport of Shanghai, with its European trading-houses. The Taipings recognised that possession of Shanghai would give them access to much-needed Western firearms and technology. Chanchufu fell in May 1860, Soochow in June, and in August the *Chung Wang* advanced towards Shanghai, where, because of the Taipings' quasi-Christian religion and the fact

that Britain and France were themselves at war with the Chinese Empire, he perhaps expected to be welcomed with open arms by the small Anglo-French garrison. However, the Taipings' reputation for perpetrating massacres wherever they went had aroused the fears of the Western community, and the *Chung Wang*'s troops were driven off when they approached the suburbs, leaving Taiping hopes of peaceful dialogue and trade with the West shattered.

In 1861 the tide again turned in favour of the Imperialists, with the recapture of Anking. This effectively cut the Heavenly Kingdom in two and set the stage for a complete recovery of Anhwei province. The mastermind of Ch'ing operations was Tseng Kuo-fan, a member of the gentry who, despairing at the inadequacies of the Manchu and Chinese regulars, had begun to organise his own army, the *Hsiang-chün*, as far back as 1853. Tseng had been raised to overall command of all government forces in the lower Yangtze theatre following the destruction of the Kiangnan barracks. It was his brother, the equally-talented general Tseng Kuo-ch'uan, who re-

Contemporary Chinese print of Taipings destroying a Buddhist temple.

took Anking in September.

A second Taiping thrust towards Shanghai in January 1862 was repulsed by the combined efforts of Imperialists and Anglo-French troops, coupled with a prolonged fall of snow. To guarantee the safety of the foreign community thereafter, the British and French authorities felt obliged to oppose the Taipings within a 30-mile radius of the city. Though their own regular troops consequently took the field on numerous occasions during 1862, both countries were reluctant to become too directly involved in the conflict, and favoured strengthening the Imperialists by providing them with military instructors and Western arms. The British, therefore, openly supported a Western-officered mercenary force, Frederick Ward's Ever-Victorious Army, or EVA (whose existence they had previously opposed) and in 1863 they even provided it with a new commander, Charles Gordon. The EVA fought mostly within the 30-mile zone round Shanghai and, while it was certainly not always as successful as its name might imply, its participation proved decisive in most operations in which it was involved. Several similar contingents were organised as a consequence.

Drawing of Imperialists evacuating a wounded comrade, from John **Scarth's** Twelve Years in China by a British Resident *(1860).*

With the help of the EVA, the Imperialists were able to drive back the *Chung Wang*'s forces gradually. Soochow – considered by the Taipings to be pivotal to the defence of besieged Nanking – was retaken in December 1863, Chanchufu in May 1864 and Hangchow, in neighbouring Chekiang province, in March. This left Nanking effectively isolated and with its much-reduced garrison weak from starvation, it fell when a mine breached its walls in July. By this time Hung Hsiu-ch'uan was already dead, having apparently committed suicide three weeks earlier, but his eldest son escaped, along with the *Chung Wang*. Both were subsequently captured and summarily executed.

There were still numerous Taiping armies scattered round the country. The principal of these, holding Hoochow in Chekiang, was driven out in August 1864 and destroyed the following spring as it retreated southwards. In October 1864 some 10–12,000 Taipings under the *Shih Wang* seized Changchow in Fukien province and remained at large until forced to surrender the following summer. The last organised Taiping remnants were destroyed at Chiaying in Kiangsi in February 1866. Though numerous Taipings remained at large among the Nien rebels still active north of the Yangtze, the Taiping Rebellion was over.

Statistics relating to this conflict are unreliable, but there is no question that the Taiping Rebellion was war on the largest scale the world had yet seen. A total of about 10 million troops had been involved, and as many as 600 cities had changed hands time and time again during 15 years of conflict. The populations of some districts were reduced by 40–80 per cent, and even by conservative estimates 20–30 million people are believed to have died, a total only exceeded by the bloodiest conflict in history, the Second World War.

MILITARY ORGANISATION

In the formal military organisation they had adopted by mid 1850, based on Chou and Ming antecedents, the Taipings demonstrated sophistication in comparison with other rebels. Surviving copies of their official military manual, the *T'ai-p'ing Chün-mu*, tell us that theoretically a Taiping *chün* or army corps comprised 13,156 men divided into five regiments (*shih*) of 2,500 men, plus officers. Each *shih* was divided in turn into five battalions (*leu*) of 500 men and each battalion into five companies (*tsu*) of 100, plus officers. Each company comprised five platoons (*liang*) of 25 men and a sergeant, and a platoon was made up of four squads (*wu*) of four privates and a corporal. An army therefore nominally comprised 10,000 privates (*wu-tsu*), 2,500 corporals (*wu-chang*), 500 sergeants (*liang-ssu-ma*), 125 company commanders (*tsu-chang*), 25 battalion commanders (*leu-shuai*), five regimental commanders (*shih-shuai*) and a commanding general (*chün-shuai*). In reality, however, units were often severely under- strength, and occasionally a *shih* comprised just 100 men, or sometimes only a few dozen.

Every family was expected to supply one soldier to the Taiping Army. As the number of Taiping adherents or conquered subjects grew, new army corps were established, with a new squad instituted for each additional five families, a new platoon for

each 26, and so on. Once 13,156 new families and thus new soldiers became available, the new corps had its own commander appointed and was split from its parent corps. This elasticity meant that it was possible for new armies to be created continuously. At the height of Taiping power there were 104 armies (nine of them classed as *shui-ying* or 'water regiments', serving on the inland waterways) as well as eight similarly organised but non-combatant corps based in Nanking, composed of miners, artificers and artisans, which constituted the regime's commissariat.

Composition

The majority of Taiping soldiers, and especially the officers, were initially from the provinces of Kwangtung and Kwangsi where the Rebellion began. Later many came from Fukien, Kiangsi, Hupeh, Hunan and Anhwei. The nucleus of each Taiping army consisted of long-term adherents, of whom the most dedicated were from Kwangsi, particularly the province's aboriginal Miaou hill-tribesmen. New recruits were scrupulously distinguished from the original adherents of the Society of God-Worshippers, who were considered the Taiping Army's elite. An Englishman serving with the Taipings in the 1860s, Augustus Lindley, states that the soldiers of each corps were actually brigaded according to expe-

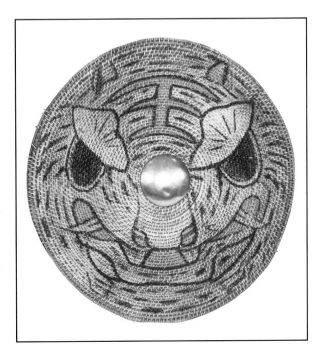

Mid 19th century Chinese shields were about three feet in diameter and made of plaited bamboo. Those of Tigermen had a matchlock barrel across the back which doubled as hand-grip. (Crown Copyright)

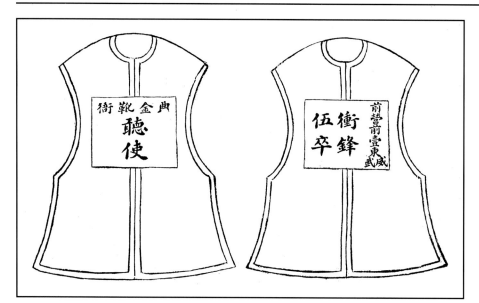

rience, either as 'bona fide Taipings' with six or more years' service, 'acknowledged brethren' with three to six years' service, or, most numerous of all, 'new levies'. In action, these three 'brigades' were further divided, the 'best and bravest' serving as musketeers and cavalry, the next bravest as jingall-men and halberdiers, and the least experienced as spearmen, who formed the front ranks.

Many Taiping soldiers served less than enthusiastically. Captured Imperialists frequently joined up simply to avoid execution and were, predictably, unreliable in the field, while after 1854 there are increasingly numerous references to 'conscripted peasants' and 'impressed villagers' as constituting a sizeable proportion of most Taiping forces. The families of such pressed men were often sent to Nanking and detained there 'as hostages for the fidelity of their male relatives in the field', while the men themselves, tattooed with the name of the Taiping dynasty on their cheeks, were closely guarded by the army's regulars. In 1860 Laurence Oliphant recorded that in action such conscripts, placed in the front ranks, were reputedly tied together by their pigtails. As some indication of numbers, 90 per cent of the Taipings who attacked Ningpo in 1861 were 'villagers pressed into their service', as were 95 per cent of those captured at Kajow in 1862.

This apparent shortage of reliable manpower was gradually compensated for during the 1860s by the incorporation of large numbers of boys, some of

them as young as six or seven. Having been indoctrinated since infancy, these were fanatical adherents of the Taiping cause. Most had been taken by force in conquered territories. Adopted and reared by army personnel, especially officers, they were 'imbued with ferocity of disposition and callousness of feeling, to execute the behests of their masters'. Several Western observers noted them being given 'privileges beyond their years' in exchange for their fidelity, and some were even commissioned as officers.

Though Taiping regulations stated that children were not to engage in active military duties, it soon became common practice for those employed by officers to accompany them into battle to reload their firearms, and by 1861 children were being fielded in ever-increasing numbers. Lindley, who considered that boys aged between 12 and 15 constituted 'the bravest soldiers and most daring spirits in the ranks of the Taiping soldiery', reckoned that in the spring of 1861 a large part of the Taiping Army consisted of 'mere boys', while R.J. Forrest, visiting Nanking in March that year, wrote that 'where there is one grown-up man there are two or three boys of from 12 to 18 years of age', adding that he 'never saw a rebel soldier who could be called old'. An account of the fighting at Chapu in September 1861 states that 60 per cent of the 5,000 Taipings involved were 'little boys', while the entire rearguard of a force that sallied out from Nanking in February 1862 consisted of boys aged between seven and 15.

Women also served in the field, mostly in menial

work such as digging trenches and constructing earthworks, but during the early Rebellion period they fought on the battlefield, organised in all-female units under their own officers. (Men and women were always rigidly segregated on active service.) Even as late as 1858, 10,000 'picked women' were still 'drilled and garrisoned in the citadel' at Nanking, but there is no evidence of women fighting after 1853.

Command structure

The *chün-shuai* commanding an army corps had only administrative and training responsibilities; in action the corps was commanded by a superintendent and a commandant. The corps commandant was the most senior military officer in the Taiping Army, but even he was often obliged to take second place to a court official, either a *ch'eng-hsiang* (chancellor), a *chien-tien* (senior secretary) or one of the 72 *chih-hui* (commanders) or 100 *chiang-chün* (court generals). In addition, before 1856 and again after 1858 there were five senior commanders called *chu-chiang*, described as having 'general control over military affairs'. One of them (the *Tung Wang* 1851–56, the *Ying Wang* 1859–62 and the *Chung Wang* 1863–64) acted as overall commander-in-chief or *chün-shih*.

There were various degrees of nobility and assorted grades of general ('Heavenly', 'Dynastic', 'Masterly' and 'Holy'), but the only title to which senior Taiping commanders truly aspired was that of *wang* or 'king'. Initially there were only six or seven of these (the *T'ien Wang* himself and his principal

associates), but the title was subsequently used as a reward for meritorious service, and as a flattery to satisfy the ambitious. Between 1856 and 1859 the number of 'kings' increased to ten, and by the end of 1861 to more than 100. Thereafter their numbers increased almost daily, with little reference to merit or ability, so that by the end of the Rebellion 2,700 had been appointed. Many undeserving officers were made *wangs* simply to avoid resentment at the promotion of others, while competent commanders were often overlooked. The *Chung Wang*, who was himself only appointed for fear that he might otherwise defect, stated that this proliferation, especially amongst Hung's own family and the despised court officials, was a principal cause of disaffection amongst Taiping officers towards the end of the Rebellion, resulting in a widespread lack of co-operation at command level.

Lindley observed that by the 1860s *wangs* had 'entire control' over the troops under their command, deeming themselves answerable only to the Heavenly King himself or to the commander-in-chief when there was one. Certainly most of those operating in outlying areas were acting all but independently of the capital by then. Finally, in 1863, Hung attempted to curb this trend by declaring that henceforth the Taiping Army was to be referred to as the 'Heavenly Army' and its soldiers as 'Royal Troops', which, the *Chung Wang* noted, 'made them all into

Manchu Bannermen, photographed in Canton by John Thomson c. 1868–72.

his personal troops and stopped us from calling them our own'. Independent action thereby became theoretically a treasonable offence.

Westerners in Taiping service

Foreign sympathisers and adventurers were to be found serving with the Taipings from 1853, most often as artillerists. Their numbers were never large, probably because the Taipings had insufficient funds to pay them regularly, but a few were seen, heard, killed or captured in virtually every engagement in Kiangsu province during 1860–64, and perhaps as many as 200 participated in the advance against Shanghai in January 1862. A troop of about 100 based at Nanking – a mixture of Englishmen, Italians, Irishmen, Americans and others, commanded by an English seaman named Savage – assisted the *Ning Wang* in successfully defending Tsingpu against Ward's Ever-Victorious Army in 1860. When Savage was killed attacking Sungkiang that August, an American named Peacock succeeded him, attaining 'high rank' among the Taipings by 1861.

Sketch of an Imperialist outpost near Peking, from the Illustrated London News *of 12 January 1861. Note the variant shape of their hats.*

Lindley, the best-known of the foreigners who fought for the Taiping cause, recorded that some even became officers in the regular Taiping Army, including a Corsican and a Sardinian army officer named Moreno, who attained the ranks of colonel (*leu-shuai*) and major respectively in one of the *Chung Wang*'s corps. An American, Henry Burgevine, who at the end of 1862 had briefly commanded the Ever-Victorious Army, was even made a *wang*.

Burgevine, and Lindley after him, both attempted to establish foreign-officered Taiping units at the *Chung Wang*'s headquarters at Soochow – the 'Americo-Taiping Legion' and the 'Loyal and Faithful Auxiliary Legion' respectively. These units were equipped with Western firearms and artillery in imitation of the EVA, but they met with little success owing to the reluctance of local commanders to supply them with enough men or sufficient firearms (the 1,000 men Burgevine had drilled by October 1863, for instance, had only 250 muskets between them). Each also stole an armed steamer for the Taipings (the *Kajow* and the EVA's *Firefly* respectively), though both were lost within a few months, Burgevine's *Kajow* being blown up in action through the clumsiness of its drunken crew.

THE IMPERIALISTS

China's military establishment – passive, parochial, weak and above all outdated – was the product of the country's a-military culture. It comprised both regular and irregular troops, the former consisting of the Eight Banners (*pa-ch'i*) and the Army of the Green Standard (*lu-ying*), and the latter of the militia (*t'uan-lien*), 'Braves' (*yung*) and, later, 'Brave Battalions' (*yung-ying*). The inadequacy of the regular elements was confirmed early in the Rebellion, and by the time the Taipings were finally crushed it was *yung-ying* forces which bore the brunt of the fighting.

The Eight Banners

The origin of the Eight Banners dated to 1601, when Nurhachu, founder of the Manchurian Ch'ing dynasty, organised his troops into four units under banners coloured respectively yellow, white, red and blue. In 1615 these units were each split in two, whence the Eight Banners. The flags of the four new units had coloured borders. Each Banner actually comprised three *kusai* or divisions – one each of Manchus, Mongols and Chinese, but the Eight Banners was essentially a Manchu army, since Manchus outnumbered the Mongols and Chinese by some three to one. Indeed, in the 19th century all living Manchus were nominally enrolled in the Banners, as were descendants of those Mongol and Chinese Bannermen who had participated in the Manchu conquest of China.

By the 19th century this hereditary soldiery, though providing large numbers, no longer constituted an effective military force. Whereas Bannermen had originally been cavalry, with an allowance sufficient to maintain between three and six horses, many now had no horse at all. They received minimal pay and often had to work in civilian jobs for their livelihood, mustering only occasionally for picturesque charades that masqueraded as drill.

Their strength appears to have been about a quarter of a million men, of whom some 50 or 60 per cent were stationed within the province of Chihli, either in or near Peking, and another 20 per cent in the principal walled towns of other provinces. The

Military mandarin visiting a guard-post. Photograph by John Thomson.

remainder were distributed in Manchuria and Turkestan. Banner garrisons outside Peking consisted of: the *Chi-fu Chu Fang*, the garrisons of the 25 cities nearest to Peking, totalling some 40,000 men, mostly infantry; the *Ling-ch'in Chu Fang* or garrisons of the Imperial Mausolea, comprising 1,250 men; and the *Ko-sheng Chu Fang*, the 25 provincial garrisons, three of which were marine establishments. The largest garrisons consisted of 4–5,000 Bannermen, the smallest of a few hundred.

Theoretically each *kusai* comprised a *tu-t'ung* (lieutenant-general) commanding five battalions (or two in a Mongol *kusai*) called *julan* or *cha-la*, each of 1,500 men. Each battalion was commanded by a *ts'an-ling* (colonel) and was organised into five companies – called *niru* in Manchu or *tso-ling* in Chinese. Each company was commanded by a major (also called a *tso-ling*). The *tso-ling* therefore nominally comprised 300 men, but was so often understrength that in 1851 it was generally considered to number

only 150, and in reality often comprised no more than 40 or 50. Lower ranking company officers were the *fang-yu* or captain, the *hsiao-ch'i hsiao* or lieutenant, and five *ling-ts'ui* or corporals. Privates were generally called *ma-chia*, technically a term indicating armoured cavalrymen, though there were also *yang-yu ping*, supernumeraries awaiting appointment to the ranks of the *ma-chia* as vacancies occurred.

This official structure had little relevance to the way Bannermen were distributed in the field, scattered in garrisons of varying sizes. Those of 3,000 or more Bannermen were usually commanded by a general bearing the title *chiang-chün* (rendered in English sources as 'Tartar General'), who in all military matters out-ranked the viceroy of whichever province he was posted to. Smaller garrisons of about 1,000 Bannermen came under a deputy lieutenant-general (*fu tu-t'ung*), and those that were smaller still were led by a commandant (*ch'eng-shou yu*).

The Peking Bannermen

The nucleus of the Banner army was the six divisions based in the capital, comprising the Imperial Bodyguard (*Ch'in-chün ying*), the Vanguard Division (*Ch'ien-feng ying*), the Flank Division (*Hu-chün ying*), the Light Division (*Ch'ien-jui ying*), the Firearms Division (*Huo-ch'i ying*) and the Paid Force (*Hsiao-ch'i ying*). The Imperial Bodyguard – a cavalry force of nearly 3,000 men – was more a ceremonial unit than a functional one. The Vanguard or Leading Division, totalling 1,500–2,000 infantry, and the 15–16,000-strong Flank Division that comprised infantry and cavalry, were both recruited among the Manchus and Mongols of all Eight Banners. The Light Division totalled 3–4,000 Chinese infantry and Mongol cavalry, while the 8,000-strong Firearms Division, again made up of Manchus and Mongols from every Banner, was organised into Inner and Outer units – for the defence of Peking and service in the field respectively.

Finally there was the Paid Force, regarded by Westerners as 'the only corps which can have any claim to be considered as an army'. Made up of some 66,000 men, this was a predominantly cavalry force (its Chinese name actually means Cavalry), of which about an eighth were Mongols and the rest roughly

Taipings (right) in action against t'uan-lien *militia.*

half and half Manchus and Chinese. It also included nearly 7,000 infantry matchlockmen, 100 sword-and-bucklermen and 100 artillerists.

In addition to these principal divisions several other units were based in Peking. The most important was the *Pu-chün ying* or Foot Force, totalling some 15,000 Manchus, 4,500 Mongols and 3,700 Chinese, plus officers, drawn from all Eight Banners. Despite its name, this division included matchlock-armed cavalry – the *Hsun-pu ying* (a mobile security force), but the majority were indeed infantry, responsible for policing the capital and guarding its walls. Other units included the *Ling-tsin ying* (the Mausolea garrison force), and the 5,800-strong *Yuan Ming Yuan* Division which protected the Summer Palace. There was also a park of some 550 artillery pieces, though less than half of these were mounted on carriages.

Matchlock-armed Bannerman, photographed by John Thomson in September 1871. Note the bamboo cartridges at his belt, containing individual measured powder charges.

A further Peking Banner division, established in 1862, was the *Shen-chi ying*. Usually referred to as the Peking Field Force, its name actually means 'Divine Mechanism Division', an allusion to the modern Western firearms with which it was equipped. This unit was unique in that it was 'drilled and manoeuvred after the European fashion', with a nucleus of Bannermen trained by the British at Tientsin. Initially about 3,000-strong, it had increased to some 6,000 men by 1865.

The Army of the Green Standard

Unlike the Eight Banners, this army (in actuality 18 individual provincial armies that varied considerably in size) consisted entirely of Chinese troops. By the 19th century it had become equally ineffective, principally through a lack of regular training, inadequate pay, widespread addiction to opium (equally rife among Bannermen) and the corruption of the vast majority of its officers. In particular, officers were guilty of filching a considerable portion of their soldiers' pay (a practice known as 'squeezing'), and of failing to keep units up to strength in order that they could pocket the pay of absentees. Indeed, some units were as much as two-thirds below their official size, and by the 1860s most were at least 40 or 50 per cent understrength, with an estimated 20 per cent of the men in many units either too old or too feeble to fight. When necessary, numbers were made up by temporarily taking on vagabonds and peasants.

Green Standard troops comprised *shou-ping* (garrison infantry), *pu-ping* (infantry) and *ma-ping* (cavalry). In most places garrison infantry outnumbered the other two put together, and *pu-ping* outnumbered *ma-ping* almost everywhere. T.F. Wade, writing in 1851, gives totals for the three categories (excluding over 7,400 officers) as some 321,900 garrison infantry, 194,800 infantry and 87,100 cavalry. Of these, only 10 per cent at most were kept regularly on active service. These figures put the overall infantry to cavalry ratio at nearly 6:1, close to the official figure of 5:1, though the *pu-ping* to *ma-ping* ratio varied between 1:1 and 10:1. In seaboard provinces up to a third of the men might be 'water soldiers' or marines, though they were still based ashore, and a small number of them were actually cavalry.

The basic unit of Green Standard organisation was the *ying* or battalion, of which there were some 1,200. Battalions were formed into brigades, called *piao* or *chen-piao*, each commanded by a *tsung-ping* (commonly called a *chen-t'ai*), or regiments (*hsieh*) commanded by a colonel (*fu-chiang*), and the number of battalions within these larger units varied. The *ying* itself nominally consisted of 500 men plus officers, but in practice could be as few as 50 men or as many as 1,000. It was commanded by a *ying-kuan* or battalion officer, usually a *ts'an-chiang* (lieutenant-

colonel) but sometimes only a major (*tu-ssu*) or captain (*shao-pei*). The *ying* was subdivided into right and left *shao* or patrols, each commanded by a lieutenant (*ch'ien-tsung*). The *shao* comprised two or four sub-units (*ssu*) under ensigns (*pa-tsung*), organised in squads (*p'eng*) of nominally ten men commanded by an NCO.

The lieutenant, ensigns and NCOs were usually commanders of the small detachments assigned to hold outposts called *hsun* (posts), *tun* or *pau* (watchtowers or lookout stations), many battalions being scattered in tiny units that might comprise no more than a dozen men. The widespread distribution of units was another factor in the decline of the Green Standard, since it was not only difficult for a commander to assemble adequate forces to cope with an unexpected emergency, but it also became virtually impossible for him to control or train his men. One *ying* on Chusan in 1860 is recorded as not having been collected for drill for the previous eight years.

The overall command structure of the Green Standard was built around a system of 'checks and balances' designed to prevent the concentration of military power with any one individual. The *tsung-ping*, for instance, was answerable to both the provincial commander-in-chief (*t'i-tu*) and the civilian governor, and although both were his seniors, they had no direct control of the bulk of the province's forces except through officers such as himself. In addition, the *tsung-ping*, *t'i-tu* and governor alike had *piao* under their own direct control, which though small units were nevertheless bigger than those of any other Green Standard commander in the province. The inevitable outcome of such fragmentation of command was disunity and a lack of co-operation.

The T'uan-lien

These were village militias, consisting of men armed mainly with spears, polearms and bows (after 1854 a few also had matchlocks) who drilled in their spare time. They were raised purely for the protection of their own communities, and were prepared to take on Imperialists as well as Taipings when the need arose. Their main value was in keeping away small bands of marauders or bandits. The *T'uan-lien* usually comprised 200–500 men at most, organised in companies of 100 and sub-units of 25 and five, though several villages together sometimes mustered a 'large *t'uan*' that could field in excess of 2,000 men. Towns had similar militia units, called *thou-ping*.

Yung and Yung-ying

Raised to compensate for the deficiencies of provincial Green Standard units, the volunteers known as *yung* or 'Braves', who drilled daily and received much higher pay than Green Standard troops, constituted a large part of most Imperialist armies by the late 1850s. Financed and sustained either by the resources of the local gentry or by officially-sanctioned local taxes, they were raised on a temporary basis whenever the need arose. Most *yung* units comprised only a few hundred men, though some totalled well over 1,000. Organisation followed similar lines to that of Green Standard units except that civilian officials were frequently appointed to command them.

The *yung-ying* or 'Brave Battalions' constituted a logical progression in the development of *yung* forces, becoming considerably larger, more permanent and subject to more rigorous selection processes and a higher standard of training. From the early

Huai Army troops on the march. Their commander is in the palanquin towards the rear.

1850s the Emperor had commissioned numerous provincial officials to raise such units. The men were recruited from the local population, and supplemented by detachments drawn from existing *t'uan-lien*, *yung* and Green Standard units. One of the earliest, and the most important, was the *Hsiang-chün*, organised in Hunan by Tseng Kuo-fan in 1853. It proved so successful that similar armies were raised along identical lines in other provinces including Anhwei (the *Huai-chün*, 1862), Chekiang (the *Ch'u-chün*, 1860), Kiangsi (the *Chiang-chün*, 1855) and Szechewan (the *Ch'uan-chün*, 1863). It was the *Hsiang-chün*, or Hunan Army, that won the Imperialists' first major victory over the Taipings in 1854, and its successes thereafter meant that from 1860, following the Taipings' decisive overthrow of the Southern Imperial Barracks outside Nanking, *yung-ying* armies eclipsed the traditional Green Standard and Banner forces and were considered not only part of the regular military establishment, but its most important part. Tseng himself eventually became governor-general and supreme commander on the lower Yangtze, responsible for not only the Hunan Army – which ultimately grew to over 130,000 men – but also for Li Hung-chang's celebrated Huai Army (60–

70,000 men) and Tso Tsung-t'ang's Chu Army (40,000 men by mid 1864).

The basic unit of all such armies was the *ying* of 500 men and six officers. The *ying* consisted of the *ch'in-ping* or battalion commander's guards (72 men organised in six platoons or *tui* of 12 men each, with two of the platoons equipped with light guns) and four *shao* of 100 men (organised in eight platoons, six of 12 men and two – equipped with jingalls – of 14; the remaining 28 men included a deputy commander, five orderlies and a cook to each *shao*). In addition, 180 coolies were attached to each *ying*, used to replace casualties in the ranks as they occurred. The *ying* was commanded by a *ying-kuan*, and the companies by *shao-kuan*. Brigades of between two and a dozen or more *ying* came under the command of a *t'ung-ling*, whose name the brigade usually took, while the command of two or more *t'ung-ling* constituted a *chün* under a *ta-shuai*.

The initial recruits were mostly farmers, preferably from a specific locality in order that they should all know one another. To ensure loyalty, *shao-kuan* were responsible for enlisting their own men; *ying-kuan* similarly chose their own *shao-kuan*, *t'ung-ling* their own *ying-kuan*, and the *ta-shuai* his *t'ung-ling*. Personal attachments were so strong that when a unit commander died his men were usually disbanded, and if he was transferred they were transferred with him. Later recruitment became less selective: size-

Lindley's depiction of the unidentified Battle of Hu-kau, in which the Taipings formed a series of circles bristling with spears to protect their musketeers against Imperialist cavalry.

able numbers of braves in the 1860s were actually ex-Taipings who had been captured or whose leaders had defected.

Waterways and paddy-fields made the countryside in which the Rebellion took place largely unsuitable for cavalry, so *yung-ying* troops were predominantly infantry. The Hunan Army's first cavalry units (organised in *ying* of 250) were only established in 1858, and the Huai Army's in 1865. However, some *ying* were specifically intended for naval service. They were organised in ten *shao* (each of one armed junk and a gunboat) plus the *ying-kuan's* larger vessel. Tseng's army before Nanking in January 1864 included 28 such river *ying*, while the Huai Army had at least 12 by August 1863.

DRESS AND WEAPONS

The Taipings

The Taipings abandoned the characteristic Manchu shaved head and pigtail, and allowed their hair to grow long over the whole head – the Imperialists referred to them as *ch'ang-mao-tsei* or 'long-haired bandits' (rendered by Western observers as 'Changmows'). It was worn either loose, tied in a knot on top of the head or twisted into a thick braid that was plaited with red or yellow silk and wound round the head with the end hanging down like a tassel at the left shoulder. (The especially long hair of the Miaou, when worn this way, was said to have been thick enough to form 'an invulnerable sort of helmet that no sword can penetrate'.) Occasionally dispensation was granted allowing certain groups – such as the sailors of the reorganised river-fleet in 1853 and elements of the population of Soochow in 1860 – to retain their pigtails, but anyone else daring to do so was beheaded out of hand. Nevertheless, several sources state that many Taipings retained their pig-

tails 'concealed beneath their flowing locks', so that should the need arise they could, by a rapid tonsure, resume the guise of loyal Imperialists.

In their dress they demonstrated a marked preference for bright colours, usually in the form of looted silks and satins; their 'tawdry harlequin garb' reputedly struck terror into those that saw it. Sometimes Kwangsi and Kwangtung veterans, by contrast, are recorded dressed entirely in sober black. Officially the Manchu custom of buttoning garments at the right side was abandoned in favour of the Ming

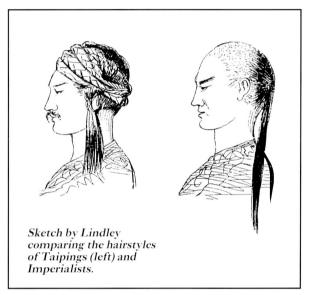

Sketch by Lindley comparing the hairstyles of Taipings (left) and Imperialists.

Lindley's drawing of the 'peculiar gaudy headdress', called a dragon-hat, worn by Taiping generals and senior officials. R.J. Forrest, a visitor to Nanking in 1861, described it as 'made of pasteboard, gilt, with amber beads and pearls suspended, and a little bird on the top', adding that it was 'only assumed on great occasions'.

front-opening, and outer jackets were supposed to be only hip-length, but pictures from that time still in existence demonstrate that such regulations were only spasmodically observed.

Only officials and soldiers were allowed to wear red jackets, though most Taipings wore a red turban or head-scarf, considered 'the distinguishing mark of a private in their army'. Yellow turbans were also worn sometimes (by female Taiping soldiers, for instance, and by the *Shou Wang*'s bodyguards), as, very occasionally, were turbans in other colours. Lindley considered the dress of a typical Taiping soldier as a red head-scarf, black silk trousers (other accounts mention red, blue or white trousers), a sash round the waist, and a close-fitting, generally red, hip-length jacket. Shoes were usually taken off, and the trousers were rolled up or tucked into the waist-band when in action. In the summer a straw coolie-hat was added.

Uniforms, comprising a coloured tunic with a contrasting edge worn over their everyday clothes, were not common among the Taipings, and were apparently limited mainly to veteran units. In the early stages of the Rebellion most were either yellow, edged in blue, green, red, black or white, or red edged in yellow, but as Taiping numbers increased other combinations were introduced (the *Chung Wang*'s men wore white uniforms edged in orange). On the breast and back were white patches (one source says they were yellow) – a 4-in. square for privates and a 5-in. square for corporals, according to the *T'ai-p'ing Chün-mu* but according to pictorial sources, actually about twice that size. The bearer's rank and unit were inscribed on the front patch and 'holy warrior' on the back. Such patches were also sometimes worn on the everyday dress of men without uniforms. Soldiers were further identified by a small wooden or brass dog-tag suspended from the waist, giving the bearer's name, rank and unit.

Other than for uniforms, only officers were permitted to wear yellow. The most senior wore a long, often ankle-length, gown, a jacket, and a cape-like hood, all yellow. The jacket and gown were often embroidered with dragons and celestial emblems while the hood frequently had a piece of jewellery above the forehead. Officers next down in rank substituted a gown coloured purple, blue or almost any shade of red, plus a yellow jacket and either a red-bordered yellow hood or a yellow-bordered red one. Officers below them had only the differenced hood and the yellow jacket of their immediate superiors, and junior grades had just the jacket (sometimes with a broad scarlet border). Senior officers often dressed down in action to avoid being singled out by the enemy. One is recorded as having substituted a black turban for his conspicuous yellow one, another as having 'dressed in very common clothes when going out to fight'. Even the *Chung Wang* customarily wore only a quilted scarlet jacket and a scarlet turban.

The majority of Taipings were armed with no more than an eight- to 18-ft spear and a knife or sometimes a sword. Some substituted a polearm, and a few had bows. Firearms were at first uncommon and initially comprised matchlocks and jingalls. The

Drawing of a Taiping wang and standard-bearer, from the binding of Lindley's Ti-Ping Tien Kwoh. *The* wang *wears what Forrest calls an 'undress' version of the dragon-hat, 'something between a mitre and a fool's cap'. W.H. Medhurst (1854) describes it as red, decorated with 'tinsel and embroidery'.*

Imperialist mandarins and soldiers, from the Illustrated London News. *Note the Tigerman on the right attired in black-striped yellow costume. Their function was to frighten the enemy by 'their wild appearance, shouts and gesticulations', as well as by scattering fireworks under his feet. Tigermen appear to have been Bannermen and there were never many of them (Laurence Oliphant stated that there were only about 20 in each of four regiments he saw in 1858).*

latter was the English name for the *t'ai-ch'iang*, a species of heavy, large-calibre matchlock with a barrel up to ten ft long that was crewed by two to five men and fired from a rest – usually a tripod or a man's shoulders; its shot weighed between four ounces and two pounds and it had a range of at least 1,000 yards. Western firearms were acquired from about 1853, and by the 1860s were found in considerable numbers; some authorities specifically attribute Taiping successes in 1857 and 1860 to their acquisition of sizeable numbers of foreign arms. In October 1863 a quarter of the defenders of Soochow possessed foreign muskets and rifles, as did nearly a third of the force that attacked Tsingpu and Sungkiang in May 1862. On the other hand, the Taiping army approaching Shanghai in January 1862 had not more than one musket between ten men.

The Taipings' few cavalrymen – often riding with their heels rather than their toes in the stirrup – were armed principally with lances and firearms, the latter a mixture of light matchlocks, Western muskets, pistols and even revolvers when they could get them (delighting especially in 'huge double-barrelled pistols', according to Lindley). However, in their most celebrated action, when just 100 routed two EVA regiments at Waissoo in 1864, they were armed only with a sword in each hand.

The Imperialists

Everyday Chinese clothes were sober in colour – mostly blue, white, brown and grey. Like the Taipings, Imperialist soldiers normally wore civilian attire under their uniform jackets, though sometimes a unit was also provided with trousers and/or shirts, usually blue or white. The uniform jacket, sleeved or sleeveless, was most commonly blue edged in red or red edged in white, though numerous other combinations were worn. (Green Standard troops seen in 1855 wore black edged in red; brown edged in pink was worn by Bannermen at the Taku Forts in 1858; Huai Army troops in 1862 wore purple edged in yellow; and Peking Bannermen at Paliakao in 1860 wore yellow edged in black.)

A circular cloth patch about 10 ins across, usually white, was generally worn on the breast and back of the jacket, standing out so prominently that one observer humourously suggested they were 'possibly designed for the enemy to aim at'. Upon these were inscribed details of the wearer's unit. Sometimes these details were put directly onto the jacket (there is one record of this from 1860 and it became an increasingly common practice in the 1870s). In common with the Taipings, the Imperialists wore a wooden dog-tag at the belt. It bore the soldier's name, age, birthplace, unit, and date of enlistment. Other paraphernalia normally attached to the belt included a purse, a tobacco-pouch, a chopstick-case and a fan-case. Every Imperialist soldier possessed a pipe and a fan (cavalrymen carried them in their boots), plus carried an umbrella across his back.

Soldiers had to provide their own footwear, usually felt-soled slippers, replaced by wooden-soled shoes for wet weather; in summer they wore bare feet or straw or leather sandals. Cavalrymen, however, invariably wore black 'Tartar boots'.

For headwear, Green Standard troops and Bannermen wore a round silk hat, with a black turned-up brim and red crown. Banner cavalrymen attached to its crown a pair of tails, variously described as being cat, fox, marten, mink or squirrel. Braves wore a turban, with their pigtail wound round the head beneath it, while militia troops are normally described as wearing bamboo coolie-hats, sometimes painted. Turbans were of a standard colour in each unit. In Kiangsu in 1862–63 the Huai Army troops wore mostly blue, red or black turbans; braves from Szechewan and Yunnan provinces operating in the

former wore predominantly yellow, dark blue and scarlet in 1861; and Imperialist troops in Kwangtung in 1854, Chekiang in 1860 and Fukien in 1861 all wore white. Chinese pictures from the time often portray Hunan and Huai Army soldiers wearing the round silk hat of regular troops, so this may have come into use alongside the turban as the importance of *yung-ying* troops to the conflict became acknowledged in official circles.

Officers wore a loose, generally purplish, gauze jacket over a heavily-embroidered 'python robe' (often replaced by a plain white one for everyday use). On the front and back of the jacket was a foot-square silk panel, embroidered with different types of bird for different grades of civilian mandarin, or animals for military men. Further distinctions of rank were indicated by the quality of the belt-clasp and the colour of the decorative button fixed to the crown of the hat. Symbols of particular merit were a yellow jacket, permitted to only 50 or 60 senior mandarins, and between one and three peacock feathers worn on the hat. On campaign most wore armour to denote their status and carried at the belt a quiver containing a specific number of arrows according to the wearer's rank. Armour was of silk or cotton stuffed with silk floss, quilted to a thickness of up to two ins and reinforced with metal studs.

Like their Taiping counterparts, Imperialist soldiers' arms varied. Regulations apparently required that each man had a shield, bow, matchlock, spear and two swords, but in reality the majority were equipped with no more than a sword and a polearm or a spear – seven ft long for cavalry, or up to 14 ft for infantry – and even many of these were in poor condition (Western descriptions of Chinese arms invariably included the word 'rusty'). *Yung-ying* organisation allowed for about half the men of each battalion to be armed with a sword or a spear, and about a fifth of them each with matchlocks and jingalls. In reality they rarely had this many (Lindley reckoning that 'not one in ten' had a matchlock).

In the right hands the bow was still considered a more effective weapon than the matchlock, but those

Bannermen in action at Tanku, 14 August 1860, from R. Swinhoe's Narrative of the North China Campaign of 1860 (1861). Banner cavalrymen were prepared to fight on foot when necessary.

competent in its use tended to come from northern China, not the southern provinces where most of the Rebellion took place. Banner cavalry in particular specialised in archery, even though many also carried a matchlock. Some cavalry units were even equipped with a certain number of jingalls; at the Battle of Changkiawan in 1860 they were either carried slung between two horses, so that the tripod stand trailed along the ground, or dismantled, with the jingall carried on one horse and its stand on another.

The introduction of Western firearms began on a small scale during the 1850s, but commenced in earnest from 1861, significantly later than for the Taipings. Even then they were limited principally to the Hunan and Huai armies. The latter had at least 1,000 muskets and rifles by September 1862, 10,000 by mid 1863 and 15,000 by spring 1864. Li Hung-chang wrote that he eventually had 300–400 muskets per *ying* compared to the Hunan Army's 120. (Spears and 'Chinese lances', or tridents, still far outnum-

Summer and winter hats of Imperialist mandarins, from J.F. Davis' China (1857).

Huai Army military jacket, blue with a red border and white piping. The light patch on the breast indicates where the identification disc was once attached. (Victoria & Albert Museum)

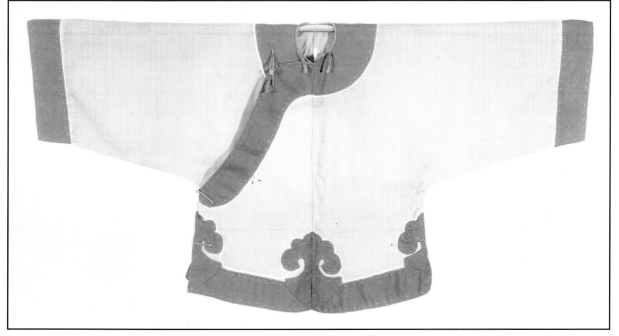

Sketch by J. Lamprey of a Huai Army jingall crew on the march, 1862.

bered muskets among the 50,000 Hunan Army men encamped before Nanking in June 1864.)

Less conventional weapons in use on both sides included magazine-fitted crossbows capable of firing eight to ten bolts in rapid succession; rockets, usually in the form of barbed arrows fitted with a firework propellant; powder-bags, containing about a pound of gunpowder and fitted with a fuse; and stinkpots – earthenware jars filled with a combustible substance which gave off asphyxiating fumes when lit.

ARTILLERY

Artillery in 19th century China differed little from that of 17th century Europe, and was often as old. The guns – usually large and heavy in relation to their calibre – were made from brass, iron, copper and even wood, occasionally ornately constructed to resemble dragons (the Taipings actually called cannons 'long dragons'). Cities and forts were provided

Imperial guns fielded against the Anglo-French in 1860.

with large quantities of artillery, mostly mounted on crude carriages without wheels or any means of depression or elevation beyond 'a lot of rough wedges'; Chinese practice was to lay their guns to fire at a point they hoped the enemy would have to pass. In consequence their fire was often highly inaccurate, and the poor quality of Chinese gunpowder and the uneven casting of their cannon-balls contributed to this 'uncertain gunnery'. Under fire, however, the Chinese stood resolutely to their guns, more often than not to the last man.

When field-artillery was called for, guns would be mounted on two-wheeled carriages that resembled hand-carts, sometimes with a curved roof, or ordinary four-wheeled carts. Most guns deployed in the field were emplaced in entrenched positions prior to battle, but by 1860 a few small-calibre Imperialist pieces were mounted on mule-drawn carriages, though as a rule, there were very few guns mounted as field-artillery. Imperialist gun-carriages appear to have been painted red if at all, with the barrels and fittings painted black; Taiping guns were probably similarly finished, though one source refers to a gun-carriage painted a 'lead colour'.

Though the Taipings possessed considerable quantities of Western and Chinese guns, as a rule they had no field artillery beyond three or four small

pieces ('rarely exceeding a 6 pdr in size') mounted on the earthworks of their numerous stockaded camps. In about 1860, however, Lindley put together a battery for the *Chung Wang* that comprised several Chinese guns and three Western pieces (a 32 pdr, an 18 pdr and a 'large French cannon') which took part in the Battle of Hu-kau.

After 1853 the Imperialists purchased much Western artillery, and they were casting imitations by 1854. From 1862 both sides also tried to copy Western explosive shells, but with limited success: Gordon noted that of those the Taipings manufactured, 'not one in 20 bursts'.

French sources noted the use of organ-guns by the Imperialists at the Battle of Paliakao. These are described as comprising a framework fitted with eight or ten jingalls that were fired either simultaneously or in succession.

Ground plan of a fortified camp by Lamprey. Each Imperialist or Taiping battalion constructed one of these for itself when operating in the vicinity of the enemy. Clusters of them were also used as outworks in the defence of cities. They usually comprised two ditches and a loopholed, sometimes palisaded breastwork, surrounded by a wide belt of knee-high sharpened bamboo stakes. Tents or reed huts were erected within, with the unit commander's facing the only gateway. The more permanent of them had additional ditches and embankments.

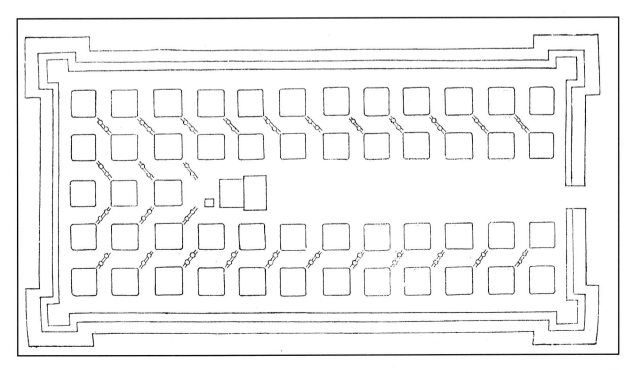

FLAGS

Chinese armies were accompanied by huge quantities of flags in assorted sizes and colours, mostly triangular but sometimes square or even, amongst the Imperialists, gonfalon-shaped. They were made of dyed silk, usually with deeply scalloped or serrated edges in a contrasting colour, fitted to a 12–13 ft bamboo pole. J. Lamprey, present in Shanghai in 1862–64, said that among the Imperialists one flag was carried per ten men, and that some were up to 12 feet long and eight feet deep. Imperialist flags were uniform to each unit and were variously described as plain, or

One of two 'snake-banners' captured from the Taipings and presented to Charles Gordon by the Emperor. (National Army Museum)

decorated with dragons, tigers, pictures of gods, 'yin and yang' symbols, clouds, circles, zig-zag lines, horizontal stripes or inscriptions. Flags of *yung-ying* forces customarily bore just the first glyph of their army commander's name.

Taiping flags appear to have been the more colourful; Westerners were dazzled by their displays of 'thousands of flags, of every colour from black to crimson'. Those of Hung Hsiu-ch'uan's original five corps were of a common colour and pattern (yellow with different-coloured borders for each corps), but as Taiping numbers grew, the colours of unit flags proliferated. Every unit leader from the sergeant upwards was accompanied by a triangular flag, the size of which increased in 6-in. increments according to his rank (from 2½ ft by 2½ ft for a sergeant up to 7½ ft by 7½ ft for a *ch'eng-hsiang*). *Wangs* and the most senior commanders substituted larger square flags. Technically they were supposed to display the officer's name, province, and unit details, but some bore religious slogans and by the 1860s it appears that many were actually plain. In addition to their formal army flags, *wangs* were also invariably accompanied by a dragon-embroidered 'snake-banner', as were senior Imperialist mandarins.

One type of Taiping flag that should be mentioned is the huge, plain black one which, once hoisted, obliged men to follow it to the death. Those who turned back were cut down by officers placed in the rear. Lindley observed that the Imperialists rarely, if ever, stood before a 'black flag' attack.

THE EVER-VICTORIOUS ARMY

The EVA was a corps of Western-trained and officered Chinese which fought for the Imperialists in the Shanghai area. Founded by an American filibuster, Frederick Ward, it started life in mid 1860 as an international battalion of about 200 mercenaries. The men were mostly deserters, runaway seamen or adventurers, predominantly American and British, though almost every country in Europe was represented in its ranks. Most were dismissed in the summer of 1861, but those kept on became officers of 1,200 Chinese soldiers that Ward had recruited in the vicinity of his headquarters at Sungkiang by Febru-

1: Taiping wang
2: Taiping spearman
3: Taiping musketeer

A

1: Manchu cavalryman
2: Imperialist matchlockman
3: Mongol cavalryman

B

1: Imperialist in winter dress
2: Small Sword rebel
3: Banner cavalryman in armour

C

The Ever-Victorious Army
1: Sergeant-Major of the Bodyguard
2: Artilleryman
3: Infantryman, summer uniform

D

1: Private, Kingsley's Force
2: 'Chinese' Gordon
3: Imperialist mandarin

E

1: Imperialist 'Brave'
2: 'Yang ch'iang tui' infantryman
3: Nien-fei cavalryman

F

Shanghai 1860-62
1: French seaman
2: Infantryman, Franco-Chinese Force of Kiangsu
3: Private, Shanghai Volunteer Corps

G

North China 1860
1: Sowar, Fane's Horse
2: Sergeant, Canton Coolie Corps
3: Private, 2nd (Queen's Royal) Regiment

H

ary 1862. Their numbers had increased to 3,000 by May, and all were equipped with Western firearms. Following its participation in the recapture of several towns the Imperialists called this new corps the *Ch'ang-sheng Chün* or 'Ever-Victorious Army', though Westerners mostly referred to it simply as 'Ward's Force'.

The British authorities in Shanghai assumed parental responsibility for the EVA during their '30-mile radius' campaign against the Taipings that spring, thereafter providing it with arms, equipment, uniforms and even drill instructors. Eventually, following Ward's death in action in September 1862, the resignation of one of his successors (Edward Forrester) only a month later and the dismissal of the next (Henry Burgevine) at the beginning of 1863, Britain also provided the EVA with its commander. A Royal Marine captain, John Holland, was temporarily appointed to the post in January, and then replaced in March by Charles Gordon of the Royal Engineers, who was subsequently nicknamed 'Chinese' Gordon.

A consular despatch dated a week after Ward's death reports that the EVA totalled some 5,000 men, but letters by Li Hung-chang between July and October 1862 generally refer to only 4,000. Another Chinese source states that in September the EVA comprised a 1st Battalion of over 1,100 men, a 2nd Battalion of under 500, a 3rd Battalion of just two companies, a Rifle Battalion of nearly 1,000, Light Artillery of 300, and Heavy Artillery of over 600 – well under 4,000 in total. After Burgevine's dismissal (which resulted from his assault on a banker who had withheld the army's pay) Li Hung-chang agreed with the British that the force should be cut to 3,000 men, but it never actually dropped below 3,500 men and often exceeded 4,000.

When Gordon assumed command he took with him a small number of British Army officers as his staff. Along with his attempts to introduce such reforms as bans on liquor and looting, this prompted widespread resentment. Consequently there were several mutinies during the first few months of his command the largest – resulting from his decision to transfer the force's headquarters to Quinsan in June 1863 – saw the departure of 2,200 men and the EVA reduced to just 1,700.

The force's numbers were restored through the

Frederick Townsend Ward (1831–1862), founder of the Ever-Victorious Army.

enlistment of Taiping prisoners. Gordon considered the Taipings 'much better men' than the ordinary Chinese, and by the end of 1863 the larger part of the EVA was made up of ex-rebels. Gordon had such confidence in their loyalty that he often fielded them against their late comrades-in-arms only days after their enlistment. However, they were consequently less well-drilled than was desirable, and by April 1864 it was reported that EVA drill and organisation were 'at a very low ebb indeed, and that the force becomes daily more ineffective'. Unsurprisingly, then, it was in the last few months of its existence that the EVA suffered most of its worst defeats. It was finally disbanded in May 1864: 104 foreign officers and 2,288 men were paid off, while about a third of the force – 600 artillery, 300 infantry and 12 officers – was transferred to the Huai Army.

Organisation

The EVA's infantry was organised into battalions, which under Gordon were more usually referred to as regiments. At full strength Ward's battalions were intended to comprise about 1,000 men, but only the 1st and Rifle Battalions appear to have ever reached this number. At both Ward's death and Burgevine's dismissal there were four battalions, but under Holland and Gordon the number increased to five, and in spring 1864 to six weaker regiments of nominally 500–600 but in effect anywhere between 350 and 650 men each. Gordon's regiments consisted of six companies, each comprising two foreign officers, seven Chinese NCOs and 80 enlisted men (though several anecdotes from 1863–64 refer to companies of 100 men). In addition there was one Chinese interpreter per regiment, though commands were given exclusively in English and had to be learnt by rote.

In addition to the infantry regiments there was a separate Bodyguard for the EVA's commander. Under Ward this consisted entirely of Manilamen (Filipinos). Their strength peaked at 200–300, but a high casualty rate (both Ward and Gordon always led their men from the front) had reduced their numbers to 50 by the time Ward died. Under Holland and Gordon, the Bodyguard comprised two distinct elements, a 'company of foreigners' consisting of 'almost every variety of the human race, from the Frenchman to the Negro', and 100 Chinamen, described as 'the elite of the Corps'.

The Artillery

The EVA's superior Western artillery, which could punch holes through the walls of stockades and cities alike, was an essential ingredient in its success. Ward is said to have assembled two 12 pdrs and several 6 pdrs as early as July 1860, and to have had two batteries by autumn 1861. However, in most actions he fielded a maximum of about a dozen pieces. Only after British involvement in the force increased following his death did artillery become more readily accessible; then guns of all shapes and sizes were made available to Holland and Gordon by the authorities in Shanghai.

By April 1863 the EVA's artillery park comprised two 8-in. howitzers, four 32-pdrs, three 24-pdr howitzers, a dozen 12-pdr howitzers, 18 12-pdr mountain-howitzers, four 8 in. brass mortars, ten 4⅖ in–5½-in. mortars, and three or six rocket-tubes, with 250–500 rounds per gun. There were six batteries, four constituting the Heavy Artillery and the remaining two the Light Artillery, with each battery consist-

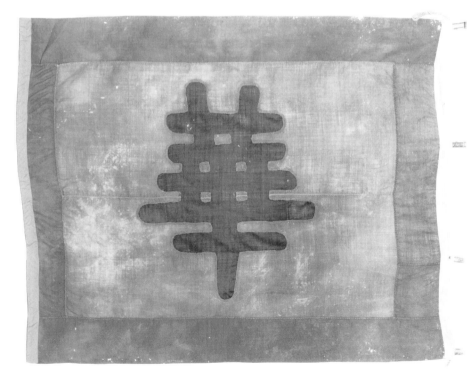

The Ever-Victorious Army's flag in Ward's time, green with a red border and the Chinese hua character – the first glyph of his name – in black. (Courtesy of Essex Institute, Salem, Mass.)

Ever-Victorious Army regiments at Quinsan, engraved from a photograph taken in December 1863.

ing, in theory, of five foreign officers, 19 Chinese NCOs and 120–150 gunners.

The river-boat fleet

After the artillery, the most important element of the EVA was its flotilla of armed paddle-steamers backed up by 30–50 Chinese gunboats. The *Chung Wang* attributed his defeat in the Soochow area almost exclusively to the EVA's paddle-steamers. (Lindley wrote that any one of them was 'more effective than a great army in the field'.) Ward bought and chartered up to a dozen, though under Burgevine their numbers were reduced to six, and under Gordon first diminished to two and were then restored to about six. The *Hyson* was the most formidable, an iron side-wheel paddle-steamer 90 ft long and 24 ft wide, with a three- to four-ft draught that allowed her to negotiate the most shallow waterways. Her armament comprised a 32-pdr in the bow and a 12-pdr howitzer in the stern, though some of the other steamers had no more than a 12-pdr bow-gun. Each was 'rendered like a movable fort' by the addition of loopholed planking round the bulwarks, designed to frustrate musketry.

The Chinese gunboats, fitted with 9-pdr or 12-pdr bow-guns, were used largely as transports (each being capable of carrying 40–50 men), but were occasionally detailed to support co-operating Imperialist forces.

OTHER 'DISCIPLINED CHINESE' UNITS

The 'Ever-Secure Army'

This unit, based at Ningpo in Chekiang, began with the raising in mid May 1862 of a force of 100 Chinamen by the local British naval commander, Roderick Dew. By September it totalled 1,000 men, organised in six companies of 150 under Royal Marine NCOs plus an artillery contingent of 50–100 men. Command was transferred to the EVA in October, and its strength reached 1,500 by amalgamation with the EVA contingent already in Ningpo. Part of this combined force was sent to Sungkiang at the end of 1862, becoming the EVA's 5th Regiment (referred to in Gordon's time as the 'Ningpo Battalion'), but 1,000 men remained in Chekiang, and in March 1863 again became independent of the EVA as the *Ch'ang-an Chün* or 'Ever-Secure Army'. Its commander was an American, James Cooke.

The original 100 men had worn white turbans, but by the time there were 300 they were already wearing green, like the EVA. After separation their uniform was described as dark blue with green facings and green turban, replaced by a white uniform with blue facings in summer.

Soldiers of Gordon's Bodyguard. (ENI Collection)

The Franco-Chinese Corps of Kiangsu

This small unit, eventually comprising 400 men plus 40 officers provided by French army NCOs, was raised in Shanghai in June 1861. It initially included an artillery element that served in the '30-mile radius' campaign with two 6-pdrs, but subsequently it appears to have become entirely infantry. Its first commander, Tardif de Moidrey, went on to become commander of the 'Ever-Triumphant Army' in January 1863, and was succeeded by Joseph Bonnefoy of the French navy. For most of its existence it operated in close co-operation either with French regular forces or as a virtual auxiliary battalion of the EVA in Gordon's time.

The 'Ever-Triumphant Army'

Jealous of the success of the British-backed EVA, the French established a similar force at Ningpo in mid 1862, with an equally exotic mixture of nationalities represented among its officers, though the majority were Frenchmen. Local Chinese merchants provided the finance, and the French authorities at Shanghai supplied instructors. Quickly known as the *Ch'ang-chieh Chün* or 'Ever-Triumphant Army', it comprised 1,200 men by the time its first commander, A.E. Le Brethon de Caligny, was killed in an attack on Showshing in January 1863. His replacement, Tardif de Moidrey, was killed attacking the same town a month later. Under Paul Neveue d'Aiguebelle, its next commander, the force was increased to some 2,500 men by May 1863. Then the provincial governor, Tso Tsung-t'ang, ordered that it be reduced to 1,500, but it was still about 1,800-strong in August 1864 when it participated in the capture of Hoochow.

The Ever-Triumphant Army and the EVA were similar in many ways. They both included a 'European Company' and a bodyguard of Manilamen; they both used armed steamers (the ETA had two by mid 1864); and they both used Western artillery, though the ETA seems to have fielded only four or five guns in most actions.

Macartney's Force

When the EVA transferred its headquarters to Quinsan in June 1863, Li Hung-chang put Sungkiang in the hands of Halliday Macartney, an ex-British Army surgeon who had been secretary to Henry Burgevine. Macartney was given the rank of colonel and assigned about 1,000 Imperialist troops with orders to 'turn them into disciplined soldiers', for which purpose he took on an unknown number of foreign officers. Known as 'Macartney's Force', this contingent also had a steamer, the *Kajow* (until it was stolen by Taiping sympathisers), along with a sizeable artillery park, comprising at least six 12-pdr howitzers and five mortars.

Kingsley's Force

This unit, based at Fahwa, consisted of Imperialists transferred to the British in June 1862 for training and placed under the command of Lieutenant Kingsley of the 67th Regiment. In October 1862 500–600 of its men saw action alongside the EVA, and in November Kingsley and his men were sent to Sungkiang to join the EVA for a proposed expedition against Nanking. By July 1863, now 1,100-strong and commanded by Lieutenant Cardew, the force was at Quinsan, and in the autumn at least part of it accompanied Gordon in the advance towards Soochow. When the EVA's 3rd Regiment, disbanded because of misconduct in August 1863, was reconstituted in October, Kingsley's force even provided the men.

ANGLO-FRENCH INVOLVEMENT

Unhappy with the Ch'ing Government's refusal to consider additional trading concessions to those agreed at the end of the Opium War, the seizure of the crew of a ship (the *Arrow*) registered in Hong Kong and the murder of a Catholic missionary by Ch'ing officials were used by Britain and France as an excuse to declare war on China in 1857. Variously referred to as the Arrow War, the Second China War and the Second Opium War, this conflict lasted, with lengthy intermissions, until 1860. Its principal actions came at the beginning and end of this period, with the capture of Canton in December 1857 and

EVA artillery practice at Quinsan. (ENI Collection)

the march on Peking in August-September 1860. Two attacks on the coastal forts at Taku – successfully in 1858 and disastrously in 1859 – constituted most of what came between. The 1860 campaign involved a sizeable Anglo-French army, but only a few thousand men were involved in the rapid sequence of victories scored at Sinho, Tangku and the Taku Forts in August, and Changkiawan and Paliakao in September.

Confusingly, at exactly the same time as they were fighting against the Imperialists in the North, Anglo-French troops stationed at Shanghai found themselves in alliance with Imperialist forces defending the city against the Taipings. Until then a shaky neutrality had been observed in China's civil war, despite the British having considered intervention on behalf of the Manchus as early as 1853. It was the Taiping threat to the sizeable Western communities in Shanghai and Ningpo, and to the trade that they represented, that finally persuaded the British and French to become actively involved, albeit only within 30 miles of each of these cities. In particular the renewal of the *Chung Wang*'s advance on Shanghai prompted a number of Anglo-French operations

The Ever-Victorious Army attacks the east gate of Fungwha, October 1862, *supported by the fieldpieces of HMS Encounter and HMS Sphinx.*

against Taiping forces in the locality between February and November 1862, notably in the so-called '30-mile radius' campaign of March-May which resulted in the recovery of ten cities for the Imperialists.

During 1860–61 garrison forces in Shanghai generally comprised some 650–1,000 British and a similar, but usually smaller, number of French troops, largely seamen and marines. After the second Taiping attack, in January 1862, however, the British element was increased dramatically, and averaged about 2,500 men until mid 1863. A substantial naval brigade was a prominent feature of this force: some 450 or more British and 300–400 French seamen and marines took part in most operations of the '30-mile radius' campaign, and their overall commanders were also naval men – Admiral Hope for the British and Admiral Prôtet (until he was killed in May 1862) for the French. Indian troops provided by the 5th Bombay Native Infantry and the 22nd Punjabis constituted another major ingredient, alongside elements of the British 31st, 67th and 99th Regiments and the French 3rd Light Infantry Battalion *d'Afrique*. Until March 1862 only a few hundred of these allied troops had actually been involved in field operations against the Taipings, but after April their numbers were increased to around 2,000. They were supported by up to 30 guns, and the British invari-

ably outnumbered the French.

In all their engagements in the Shanghai area the allies acted in concert with Imperialist forces, usually represented by the Ever-Victorious Army and occasionally local *yung-ying* forces. In allied operations in the Ningpo district, however, it was foreign-officered Chinese units such as the EVA, Roderick Dew's Ningpo force and the Ever-Triumphant Army which provided the bulk of the troops, supported by only small numbers of British and French seamen (though usually they were equipped with several artillery pieces). Gunboats were also occasionally employed in both theatres.

The Shanghai Volunteer Corps

In 1861–62 it was anticipated that the Western community in Shanghai could, in an emergency, muster some 4–5,000 men, about half of whom would come from regular troops and naval brigades as outlined above, with the balance made up from the crews of merchant ships and the volunteers who constituted the Shanghai Volunteer Corps. This force had first been organised by British and American residents in April 1853, for self-defence during the disturbances resulting from the Small Sword uprising. It was disbanded following the defeat of the rebels in 1855 but revived in June 1861 in response to the increasing risk of Taiping attack. By then its membership was largely Anglo-French but with 'a plentiful sprinkling' of Americans. There were 150 volunteers by August and 'some hundreds' by the end of 1861, organised in companies of about 50 men. They saw action only once, against unruly Imperialist troops in the so-called 'Battle of Muddy Flat' in April 1854, in which 50 British and 25 American volunteers took part alongside an Anglo-American naval brigade. However, during the Taiping attack on Shanghai in January 1862 they performed the duty of 'guarding nightly the inner line of defences'. They were initially equipped with a smoothbore musket and bayonet, which were later replaced by a rifle and sword.

Charles Gordon in the costume of a mandarin. The flags in the background are probably his own as commander of the Ever-Victorious Army. One is a red dragon-banner; the other, green edged in red with a black inscription, is perhaps the one described as bearing the names of his victories in Chinese characters.

A 30-strong cavalry troop called the Shanghai Mounted Rangers was added in December 1861. This provided Admiral Hope with scouts during the allied operations round Shanghai in 1862, and became involved in a skirmish with Taiping marauders in August. Though initially mounted on horses, they very soon changed to native ponies. They were apparently armed with sabres and firearms.

CHINESE TACTICS

Though Westerners considered the Chinese timid, it would be fairer to describe them as supremely cautious; they saw nothing meritorious in heroics or self-sacrifice. 'They have a maxim that "rash and arrogant soldiers must be defeated",' wrote John Davis in the 1830s, 'and the chief virtue of their strategy is extreme caution and love of craft, not without a large share of perfidy and falsehood.' Another observer

wrote that Chinese soldiers did not consider themselves to have 'any self-respect to lose, or credit to gain', so that even headlong flight brought no disgrace, and as soon as the scare was over they were ready to fight again. Nevertheless, Western officers repeatedly remarked on a lack of resolution among Chinese in the field and of their preference for overawing the enemy by numbers, quantity of flags, size of guns and volume of noise, rather than by actively engaging in combat.

On the battlefield they would send out a cloud of skirmishers armed with jingalls, swords and shields, while the rest of the army advanced in parallel columns. The latter would wheel into line of battle when nearing the enemy, usually in three to five

individual bodies arrayed crescent-like to threaten the enemy's front and flanks simultaneously. When available cavalry formed the wings or the reserve, and artillery was either massed in the centre or distributed along the entire front. The Taipings placed their poorest troops – usually spearmen – in the front ranks and their veterans and guard-units in the rear, probably because the Imperialist front ranks usually consisted of matchlockmen and archers. Troops on both sides manoeuvred to signals transmitted by drums, gongs and flag movements.

They often opened fire long before the enemy came into range, hoping to scare them off. This barrage would then, in theory, be followed by a general advance, coupled with an attempt at encirclement by the flank detachments. In hand-to-hand combat the Taipings were recognised to have an advantage; Imperialists preferred to stand off and duel with firearms from a distance. Lindley noted that whenever the Taipings managed to get to close quarters they were victorious, even against foreign-officered Imperialists such as the EVA. However, by the 1860s they were rarely able to close with the enemy before 'overwhelming artillery and regular

Engagement between the armed steamer Ti-ping *(the ex-EVA* Firefly*), commanded by Augustus Lindley, and a flotilla of Imperialist gunboats, November 1863. The strategic importance of the Yangtze and its tributaries meant that both sides maintained*

sizeable river navies. Gunboats constituted the larger part of these, crewed by ten to 20 or more men depending on size and equipped with a bow-gun that could be anything from a 4 pdr to a 24 pdr, with a second gun sometimes fitted at the stern.

Soldiers of the Ever-Secure Army at Ningpo, photographed by John Thomson.

volleys of musketry' mowed them down. Consequently, neither side usually charged head-on, preferring feints and skirmishes, which is why battles frequently deteriorated into sham fights in which both sides carefully avoided contact. Attackers confronted by an enemy who stood firm would fall back, often in good order, and retreat by companies, firing as they went; then an exchange of musketry would be resumed. A second advance might follow but if this too failed the entire army might quit the field. If no headway were made by either side, both would withdraw, 'each proclaiming the extermination of the other'. Defeated troops were generally pursued at a safe distance, however, since in the early part of the Rebellion the Taipings several times succeeded in drawing unwary Imperialists into ambushes by feigning flight.

When confronted by cavalry, infantry would form up in circles. Lindley witnessed the *Chung Wang*'s entire army draw up in two rows of staggered circles, bristling with spears and halberds. The first row contained musketeers and the second jingalls, and they successfully withstood the determined

charge of several thousand Banner cavalry. The musketeers maintained a continuous fire by 'running round and round . . . loading as they passed towards the rear of the circle and firing as they came to the front'.

In most battles one side or the other was usually in an entrenched position, from which Chinese troops fought with far more determination than when in the open field. In the closing stages of the Rebellion the Taipings in particular depended heavily on their field-works, and the Imperialists rarely attacked them successfully unless supported by the foreign-officered contingents with their powerful Western artillery.

THE PLATES

A1: Taiping wang
Wangs mostly wore yellow and red. Though depicted on foot here, they were mounted on the battlefield, and their standard-bearers, invariably on foot, had to run to keep up with them.

41

A2: Taiping spearman

The greatest number of Taiping spears by far were simply an iron spike fitted to a bamboo pole. A short, heavy sword akin to a cutlass was often carried as secondary armament, either stuffed through the waist-sash or slung across the back in a scabbard.

A3: Taiping musketeer

This man is armed with a British 'Tower' musket. The Taipings usually obtained their Western firearms from unscrupulous Shanghai traders (mostly Americans) unable to resist the 'fabulous sums' – up to $100 for a single musket – offered for even very inferior arms. Documents seized from one such trading-house in 1862 showed that during ten months it had supplied over 3,000 muskets, rifles and shotguns, 18,000 cartridges and over four-and-a-half million percussion caps, as well as several hundred guns. However, the arms were generally of poor quality, either old and worn or badly made.

In his left hand is a painted wicker or bamboo 'victory helmet', which Taiping regulations stated could only be worn in battle. It is never mentioned in Western sources so was probably rarely used.

An element of the Franco-Chinese Corps of Kiangsu, from the Illustrated London News, *29 August 1863. The officer is probably Joseph Bonnefoy.*

B1: Manchu cavalryman

Most Banner cavalrymen were armed with spear and bow or matchlock, or all three. The quiver and bowcase were carried either slung across the back or suspended from the waist. The quiver contained 27–60 arrows of three different types. A bare sword was frequently secured under the saddle-flap. Cavalry ponies came from Mongolia and Manchuria and averaged 12½–14 hands. They were sometimes uniform in colour within a unit: two battalions seen in 1858 were mounted respectively on white and piebald horses.

B2: Imperialist matchlockman

The Chinese matchlock had only a short, angled grip like a pistol, and was fired held against the chest, the cheek, or the right side at about hip-height. It was not very accurate except at close range (largely through insufficient practice) and the small bullets it fired – mostly cylindrical slugs rather than spherical balls, used up to six or ten at a time – had little penetrative power. Powder was carried either in a lacquered wooden flask or as prepared charges in the form of paper cartridges or small bamboo containers that were emptied down the barrel. No wadding was used, nor was the rammer; bullets were sent home by striking the butt of the piece against the ground.

B3: Mongol cavalryman

Mongol cavalry were frequently employed during emergencies, especially those of the Chahar tribe, which could field over 8,000 men. (In theory the Mongols could muster a quarter of a million cavalry, but in practice, only less than a tenth of this number.) Organisation was in *koshun* or 'standards', made up of about ten *tso-ling*, each of nominally 150 men but usually understrength. Like the Chinese, Mongols shaved the front of the head and wore their hair in a pigtail. Outer clothes were chiefly of tanned leather and sheepskin, worn over baggy trousers and a cotton kaftan that was usually blue. Armament consisted of a long spear, bow, matchlock and sword.

C1: Imperialist in winter dress

To cope with cold weather the Chinese wore up to a dozen coats one over another. The outermost would preferably be of sheepskin or fur. A pair of quilted leggings was pulled on over the trousers and secured to the girdle by loops. Such multiple layers would occasionally stop even a rifle bullet.

C2: Small Sword rebel

The Small Sword Society seized Shanghai in September 1853 and held it until February 1855 (when French troops assisted the Imperialists in its recapture). They flew Taiping as well as Triad flags but received no military assistance from the former, whose sphere of influence did not by then extend east of Nanking. The majority wore red turbans and abandoned the pigtail, wearing their long hair 'gathered up into a knot on the crown'. John Scarth records that their dress betrayed Western influence, with pockets, gloves and leather belts; some even wore English shoes and socks. Many had Western firearms, including Minié rifles and Colt revolvers.

C3: Banner cavalryman in armour

Armour was still worn by some Bannermen and most officers, more as a military insignia than a form of defence. It consisted of decoratively embroidered quilted cotton (silk for officers), reinforced with iron or brass studs. It was called *ting kia* or 'armour with nails', and occasionally still incorporated a lining of small metal plates. Among Banner cavalrymen the

Frenchmen of the Ever-Triumphant Army, engraved from a contemporary photograph.

colour of the quilted fabric was uniform within a unit. Helmets were of steel or leather, often painted or otherwise decorated, with a tall plume tube that usually bore a tuft of red horsehair or a small red flag.

The Ever-Victorious Army

D1: Sergeant-Major of the Bodyguard

Though several contemporary photographs exist, the only full description of EVA uniform colours comes from the *North China Herald* of 31 January 1863, which tells us that the Bodyguard wore 'blue with scarlet facings, and green shoulder straps bearing their designation in Chinese characters'. The entire army wore green turbans, which earnt them one of their two Chinese nicknames, 'green-headed braves'. (The other, 'imitation foreign devils', alluded to their Western-style uniforms.) The EVA's few Chinese company commanders were promoted from among its sergeant-majors.

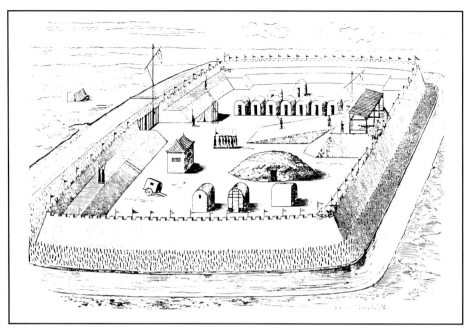

Diagrammatic representation of a Chinese fort of the sort that guarded the Peiho at Taku, from Escayrac de Lauture's Memoires sur la Chine *(1865).*

Right: The interior of the North Fort at Taku after capture, 21 August 1860, engraved from one of Beato's famous photographs.

D2: Artilleryman

The Artillery's winter uniform was light blue, with scarlet shoulder-straps and facings and a broad scarlet stripe down the trouser-leg. Though some EVA soldiers wore Western boots, artillerymen, without exception, wore Chinese slippers and stockings.

D3: Infantryman, summer uniform

The winter uniform of the Infantry was dark green, with scarlet facings, and shoulder-straps that were a different colour for each regiment and 'stamped' with the regiment's number in Chinese and English. In the summer Infantry, Artillery and Bodyguard alike changed into 'a complete white uniform with red facings, precisely similar to the *kahkee* dress worn by British troops in India'. The blanket-roll, worn all year round, is described in 1862 as coming in 'all manner of bright colours'. His weapon is a smoothbore percussion musket. Only the 4th or Rifle Regiment was equipped with rifles – either Enfields or Dreyse needle-guns.

E1: Private, Kingsley's Force

This figure is from a sketch by Lamprey, who describes their uniform as being of blue serge, worn with a turban that could be black, red or light blue. Lindley tells us that they had the number '67' on their shoulder-straps – the regiment to which their British officers belonged. Most of the force was armed with percussion muskets, but a few had Enfield rifles.

E2: 'Chinese' Gordon

The dress of EVA officers was varied. Certainly a uniform existed by April 1861, perhaps the same blue jacket, trousers and cap as comprised the uniform of the force while it was still entirely composed of foreigners. However, one sinologist, H.B. Morse, wrote earlier this century that officers wore green uniforms with black braid round the cuffs. Photographs show jackets similar to a British Army patrol-jacket or frock-coat. American officers in particular, however, appear to have remained un-uniformed, wearing 'buccaneering, brigand-like dress . . . striped, armed and booted like theatrical banditti'. Ward wore no uniform; instead he usually wore either a dark blue English frock-coat and a short cape, or a loose, blue serge tunic. Gordon wore his own RE undress uniform.

E3: Imperialist mandarin

The tiger on his embroidered chest panel and the blue button on his hat indicate that this is a fourth-grade military mandarin. Officers of this seniority were rarely found anywhere near the battlefield. (Westerners noted that the more exalted their rank the faster they retired to the rear; only the most junior were normally found in the firing line.)

F1: Imperialist 'Brave'

This figure, from another Lamprey sketch, depicts the characteristic appearance of such irregulars, typified by the large turban and the gaitered or bandaged shins and bare feet.

F2: 'Yang ch'iang tui' infantryman

This is an infantryman of the Huai Army's *yang-ch'iang tui* or 'foreign arms platoons', trained and occasionally led by foreign officers. Unlike most Taipings, such Imperialist units adopted the bayonet along with their Western firearms, carrying it fixed to the musket at all times since they possessed no scabbards.

F3: Nien-fei cavalryman

The 'Nien bandits', rebels active mainly in Shantung, Honan, Anhwei and Kiangsu provinces, co-operated with the Taipings intermittently from 1853; some of their leaders were even appointed *wangs*. Their strength lay in the sizeable cavalry that they could field by the late 1850s (totalling on average 20,000 men after 1860), mainly armed with swords

and long bamboo lances, though some had firearms. Infantry were also armed predominantly with long spears, but they also carried swords and jingalls, and had both field-guns and heavy artillery. Initially some Nien wore uniforms (reported in 1854 to have been copied in colour and style from the Taipings), but these were in a minority. All wore their hair long, covered with a red or yellow turban. Chiefs wore brown or red jackets.

Shanghai 1860–62

G1: French seaman

Seamen and marines provided the bulk of the French troops who took part in the '30-mile radius' campaign of spring 1862. They also participated in operations against the Imperialists in 1857–60, notably the capture of Canton.

G2: Infantryman, Franco-Chinese Force of Kiangsu

We know with certainty only that this unit wore turbans striped in blue, white and red (as did the Ever-Triumphant Army), though it is clear from the only known picture that their jackets were white. The other colours are hypothetical, albeit likely.

G3: Private, Shanghai Volunteer Corps
Volunteers were responsible for providing their own uniform, which appears to have comprised a red shirt and white trousers in summer, a skirted red jacket and black trousers with a red stripe in winter, and a black trilby with cock-feather plume. However, photographs taken in the 1870s indicate that elements of summer and winter uniforms were often worn together.

North China 1860

H1: Sowar, Fane's Horse
Fane's Horse was one of two Sikh cavalry regiments that served in this campaign. The other was Probyn's, whose uniform comprised a dark blue-grey tunic, red cummerbund, slate-coloured turban and white breeches. Both regiments were armed with pistols, carbine, lance and tulwar.

French attack on the bridge at Paliakao, 21 September 1860.

H2: Sergeant, Canton Coolie Corps
The Canton or Chinese Coolie Corps was raised in 1857. Some 2,500 served in North China, carrying their loads slung from a pole between two men. Those who could speak a little English were made NCOs. A slightly different uniform was worn in 1857–59, with 'Military Train' on the hat and the unit details on a diagonal white sash rather than patches on the breast and back.

H3: Private, 2nd (Queen's Royal) Regiment
This figure is based on the drawings of H.H. Crealock. The Chinese are said to have nicknamed British infantrymen 'Hats' in reference to their distinctive white airpipe helmets. Similar helmets were worn by some French troops during this campaign, and there exists a picture of the attack on the Taku Forts showing them being worn by French gunners.

Recommended Reading
W.L. Bales *T'so Tsungt'ang* (1937); Lindesay Brine, *The Taeping Rebellion in China* (1862); Holger Cahill, *A Yankee Adventurer* (1930); Prescott Clarke and J.S. Gregory, *Western Reports on the Taiping* (1982); C.A.

Drawing by Scarth of Small Sword rebels at Shanghai, 1853–55.

Curwen, *Taiping Rebel* (1977); William Hail, *Tseng Kuo-fan and the Taiping Rebellion* (1927): A. Egmont Hake, *Events in the Taeping Rebellion* (1891); Jen Yu-wen, *The Taiping Revolutionary Movement*, (1973); Augustus F. Lindley, *Ti-Ping Tien Kwoh* (1886); Thomas Meadows, *The Chinese and their Rebellions* (1856); Richard J. Smith, *Mercenaries and Mandarins* (1978) and 'Chinese Military Institutions in the Mid-Nineteenth Century', *Journal of Asian History*, vol VIII, (1974); Stanley Spector, *Li Hung-chang and the Huai Army* (1964); T.F. Wade, 'The Army of the Chinese Empire', *The Chinese Repository*, vol XX (1851); Andrew Wilson, *The 'Ever-Victorious Army'* (1868).

Notes sur les planches en couleur

A1 Un wang de Taiping à pied habillé en jaune et rouge. Les Wangs étaient généralement à cheval sur le champ de bataille. A2 Taiping armé d'une lance. Il porte une lance constituée d'une pinte en fer montée sur du bambou. Ils portaient aussi souvent une petite épée lourde, qui était en bandoulière sur le dos ou dans la ceinture. A3 Ce mousquetaire Taiping porte un mousquet 'Tower' britannique, sans doute acheté à grands frais à un marchand de Shanghai. A la main gauche il a le 'casque de la victoire' en vannerie/bambou peint. Les règlements Taiping stipulaient que ces casques pouvaient seulement être portés durant le combat.

B1 Ce cavalier Manchu porte une épée et un fusil à mèche. Des épées et des arcs étaient également parfois portés. Les chevaux de cavalerie venaient de Mongolie et de Mandchourie et avaient en moyenne 12 1/2 à 14 mains de haut Dans certains cas une unité adoptait une couleur d'uniforme pour ses chevaux. B2 Impérialistes armés d'un fusil à mèche de style chinois. Ces fusils avaient une petite gâchette inclinée et n'étaient précis qu'à courte portée. La poudre se trouve dans le flacon en bois et les cartouches dans la ceinture. Les petites balles cylindriques étaient mises en place en frappant la crosse du fusil sur le sol. Ils n'utilisaient ni d'étoupe ni de pilon. B3 les mongols se rasaient le front et portaient une queue de cheval. Cet homme porte du cuir tanné et une peau de mouton par dessus un pantalon large. Il est armé d'une longue lance, d'un arc et fusil à mèche et d'une épée.

C1 Impérialist, uniforme d'hiver. Les chinois portaient jusqu'à douze manteaux, l'un par dessus l'autre. Ils portaient alors des caleçons matelassés par dessus leur pantalon. C2 Rebelle 'petite épée'. Son apparence est influencée par l'Occident, par exemple les poches sur le manteau, les gants et les chaussures. Ces rebelles portaient souvent des armes occidentales, y compris des fusils Minié et des revolvers Colt. C3 Cavalier porte-enseigne en armure. L'armure (en coton matelassé renforcé de clous de fer ou de cuivre et quelquefois doublée de petites plaques métalliques) était à cette époque portée comme insigne et non plus comme protection. Le casque est en acier.

D L'Armée victorieuse D1 Sergent-Major des Gardes du Corps. Toute l'armée portait un tuban vert, qui lui valut le surnom de 'braves à la tête verte'. D2 Artilleur en uniforme d'hiver bleu ciel avec des épaulettes et des parements écarlates. Certains soldats EVA portaient des bottes occidentales mais tous les artilleurs portaient des pantoufles et des bas chinois. D3 Soldat d'infanterie en uniforme d'été, blanc aux parements rouges. Il porte un sac à couvertures et porte un mousquet à percussion à canon lisse.

E1 Soldat du rang, Kingsley's Force, qui porte un uniforme en serge bleu et un turban noir. Les hommes de cette force étaient armés avec soit des fusils Enfield soit des mousquets à percussion. E2 Gordon 'Chinois'. L'uniforme des officiers EVA était varié, mais en avril 1861 un uniforme (sans doute la même veste, le pantalon et let calot bleus portés par le reste des troupes) fut adopté. E3 Le tigre sur le plastron brodé de cet homme et le coton bleu sur son chapeau indiquent qu'il est un mandarin militaire de quatrième rang. Les officiers de ce rang étaient rarement vus près du champ de bataille.

F1 L'apparance de ce 'brave' impérialiste est typique de ces irréguliers. Il porte un grand turban, ses mollets sont bandés et il a les pieds nus. F2 Ce soldat d'infanterie du Yang ch'iang tui aurait été formé et peut-être dirigé par des officiers étrangers. A la différence de la plupart des Taipings son armée adopta la baïonnette mais comme ils n'avaient pas de fourreau ils la portaient toujours fixée. F3 Les bandits Nien étaient actifs dans les provinces de Shantung, Honan, Anwhei et Kiangsu. Leur force était leur cavalerie: plus de 20.000 hommes après 1860. Les cavaliers étaient armés de longues lances, épées et jungalls. Dans l'ensemble, les Nien ne portaient pas d'uniforme mais ils avaient tous les cheveux longs et couverts d'un turban rouge ou jaune.

G1 Les marins français comme celui-ci participèrent à la campagne '30-mile radius' au printemps 1862 et participèrent également à des opérations contre les Impérialistes en 1857–60. G2 Soldat d'infanterie, force franco-chinoise de Kiangsu portant le turban bleu, blanc et rouge de l'unité. G3 Ce soldat du rang, du Shanghai Volunteer Corps aurait eu la responsabilité de fournir son uniforme: chemise rouge et pantalon blanc en été, veste rouge à basque et pantalon noir avec une rayure rouge en hiver plus un trilby noir avec un panache en plumes. Mais quelques indices donnent à penser que les éléments d'uniforme d'été et d'hiver étaient portés ensemble.

H1 Sowar de Fane's Horse, l'un des deux régiments de cavalerie Sikh qui servirent durant cette campagne. Ces deux régiments étaient armés de pistolets, carabine, lances et tulwar. H2 Sergent du Canton Coolie Corps. Quelque 2500 hommes servirent en Chine du Nord, portant leur matériel suspendu à une perche entre deux hommes. H3 Soldat du rang du 2nd (Queen's Royal) Regiment. Illustration inspirée des dessins de H.H. Crealock. Les chinois surnommèrent les soldats d'infanterie britanniques 'hats' à cause des casques bien reconnaissables qu'ils portaient.

Farbtafeln

A1 Ein "Wang" der Taiping zu Fuß in gelb-roter Kleidung. In die Schlacht zogen die Wangs für gewöhnlich zu Pferde. A2 Dieser Speerträger der Taiping hat einen Speer bei sich, dessen Eisenspitze an einem Bambusstab befestigt ist. Oft trugen diese Männer außerdem ein kurzes, schweres Schwert, das entweder über der Schulter getragen oder in die Taillenschärpe gesteckt wurde. A3 Dieser Musketier der Taiping hat eine britische "Tower"-Muskete, die er wahrscheinlich für viel Geld bei einem Händler in Schanghai erstanden hat. In seiner linken Hand hält er den bemalten "Siegeshelm" aus Korbgeflecht/Bambus, Laut der Vorschriften der Taiping durfte dieser Helm nur in der Schlacht getragen werden.

B1 Deiser Kavallerist aus der Mandschurei hat einen Speer und eine Luntenmuskete bei sich. Außerdem führte man Schwerter und Bogen mit. Die Ponys der Kavallerie stammten aus der Mongolei und der Mandschurei und waren ungefähr 12 1/2 bis 14 Handbreit groß. In einigen Fällen hatten bestimmte Einheiten jeweils Ponys der gleichen Farbe. B2 Deiser Imperialist ist mit einer Lutenmuskete chinesischen Modells bewaffnet. Diese Gewehre hatten einen kurzen, abgewinkelten Griff und waren nur bei geringer Schußweite zielsicher. Das Schießpulver wurde in hölzernen Flächchen getragen, die Patronen wurden im Gürtel verstaut. Die kleinen, zylinderförmigen Kugeln wurden durch Aufstoßen des Gewehrkolbens auf dem Boden geladen, und man bediente sich keiner Pfropfen order Stampfer. B3 Die Mongolen rasierten sich den Vorderkopf und trugen ihr Haar in einem Pferdeschwanz. Dieser Mann trägt gegerbtes Leder und Schaffell über den weit geschnittenen Hosen. Er ist mit einem langen Speer, Bogen, Luntenmuskete und einem Schwert bewaffnet.

C1 Imperialist in Winterkleidung. Die Chinesen trugen bis zu zwölf Jacken übereinander. Über die Hosen zog man wattierte Beinkleider. C2 Die Kleidung der "Small Sword"-Rebellen zeigt deutlich westliche Einflüsse, zum Beispiel die Taschen an der Jacke, die Handschuhe und die Schuhe. Die Rebellen hatten oft westliche Schußwaffen, unter anderem Minié-Gewehre und Colt-Revolver. C3 Bannerträger der Kavallerie in Rüstung. Die Rüstung (aus wattiertem Baumwollstoff, der mit Eisen- bzw. Messingnieten verstärkt und manchmal mit Metallblättchen gefüttert war) trug man inzwischen eher als Rangabzeichen als zum Schutz. Der Helm ist aus Stahl.

D Die "Ever-Victorious Army" (EVA) – "Stets Siegreiche Armee". D1 Hauptfeldwebel der Leibwache. Die gesamte Armee trug grüne Turbane, was ihr den Beinamen "grünköpfige Krieger" einbrachte. D2 Artillerist in der hellblauen Winteruniform mit purpurroten Schulterklappen und Blenden. Einige Soldaten der EVA trugen westliche Stiefel, doch sämtliche Artilleristen trugen chinesische Pantoffeln und Strümpfe. D3 Infanterist in der weißen Sommeruniform mit roten Blenden. Er hat eine aufgerollte Felddecke und eine Perkussionsmuskete mit glattem Lauf bei sich.

E1 Gefreiter der Kingsley's Force in der blauen Serge-Uniform und schwarzem Turban. Die Männer dieser Truppe waren entweder mit Enfield-Gewehren oder Perkussionsmusketen ausgerüstet. E2 "Chinesischer" Gordon. Die Kleidung der EVA-Offiziere war recht unterschiedlich, doch wurde im April 1861 eine Uniform eingeführt, die wahrscheinlich aus der gleichen blauen Jacke, Hose und Mütze bestand, die der Rest der Truppe trug. E3 Der aufgestickte Tiger auf der Brust dieses Mannes und der blaue Knopf auf seinem Hut machen ihn als Militärmandarin des vierten Grades erkenntlich. Offiziere diesen hohen Dienstgrades waren recht selten in der Nähe des Schlachtfeldes anzutreffen.

F1 Der Aufzug dieses Imperialisten-"Kriegers" ist für solch Irreguläre typisch. Er trägt einen großen Turban, seine Schienbeine sind bandagiert/mit Gamaschen versehen, und er ist barfuß. F2 Dieser Infanterist der Yang ch'iang tui wurde wahrscheinlich von ausländischen Offizieren ausgebildet und unter Umständen auch unter deren Kommando. Im Gegensatz zum Großteil der Taipings trug diese Truppe das Bajonett, das jedoch stets aufgesetzt mitgeführt wurde da man keine Scheiden dafür hatte. F3 Die "Nien-Banditen" waren in den Provinzen Shantung, Honan, Anwhei und Kiangsu aktiv. Ihre Stärke war die KavallerieL nach 1860 belief sie sich auf über 20.000 Mann. Die Kavalleristen waren mit langen Speeren, Schwertern und großen indischen Musketen bewaffnet. Die Nien trugen meistens keine Uniform, doch hatten sie alle langes Haar, das mit einem roten oder gelben Turban bedeckt wurde.

G1 Französische Matrogen, wie die hier abgebildete Figur, nahmen im Frühjahr 1862 am "48 km-Radius"-Feldzug teil sowie an Einsätzen gegen die Imperialisten 1857–60. G2 Infanterist der franko-chinesischen Truppe von Kiangsu im blauweißrot gestreiften Turban der Einheit. G3 Deiser Gefreite des Shanghai Volunteer Corps hätte seine eigene Uniform zu stellen, die im Sommer aus einem roten Hemd und weißen Hosen und im Winter aus einer roten Schoßjacke und schwarzen Hosen mit einem roten Streifen bestand, sowie einem schwarzen Klapprandhut mit Hahnenfeder. Doch weisen einige Quellen darauf hin, daß einzelne Teile der Sommer- und Winteruniform zusammen getragen wurden.

H1 Sowar der Fane's Horse, einem der beiden Kavallerieregimenter der Sikhs, die an diesem Feldzug beteiligt waren. Beide Regimenter waren mit Pistolen, Karabinern, Lanzen und Krummsäbeln bewaffnet. H2 Feldwebel des Canton Coolie Corps. Etwa 2.500 Männer dienten in Nordchina. Sie trugen ihr Gepäck an einem Stab, der jeweis von zwei Männern getragen wurde. H3 Gefreiter des 2. (Queen's Royal) Regiment, die Abbildung beruht auf den Zeichnungen von H.H. Crealock. Die Chinesen gaben den britischen Infanteristen den Spitznamen "Hüte" aufgrund der röhrenförmigen Helme, die sie trugen.